20 FUN FACTS ABOUT THE HANGING GARDENS OF BABYLON

BY EMILY MAHONEY

Gareth Stevens
PUBLISHING

Please visit our website, www.garethstevens.com. For a free color catalog of all our high-quality books, call toll free 1-800-542-2595 or fax 1-877-542-2596.

Library of Congress Cataloging-in-Publication Data

Names: Mahoney, Emily Jankowski, author.
Title: 20 fun facts about the Hanging Gardens of Babylon / Emily Mahoney.
Other titles: Twenty fun facts about the Hanging Gardens of Babylon | Fun
  fact file. World wonders!
Description: New York : Gareth Stevens Publishing, 2020. | Series: Fun fact
  file: world wonders | Includes bibliographical references and index.
Identifiers: LCCN 2018049564| ISBN 9781538237786 (pbk.) | ISBN 9781538237809
  (library bound) | ISBN 9781538237793 (6 pack)
Subjects: LCSH: Gardens–Iraq–Babylon (Extinct city)–History–Juvenile
  literature. | Seven Wonders of the World–Juvenile literature. | Babylon
  (Extinct city)–History–Juvenile literature. | Archaeology and
  history–Iraq–Babylon (Extinct city)–Juvenile literature.
Classification: LCC DS70.5.B3 M34 2020 | DDC 935/.5–dc23
LC record available at https://lccn.loc.gov/2018049564
First Edition

Published in 2020 by
Gareth Stevens Publishing
111 East 14th Street, Suite 349
New York, NY 10003

Designer: Sarah Liddell
Editor: Kristen Nelson

Photo credits: Cover, p. 1 Universal History Archive/Universal Images Group/Getty Images;
file folder used throughout David Smart/Shutterstock.com; binder clip used throughout
luckyraccoon/Shutterstock.com; wood grain background used throughout ARENA Creative/
Shutterstock.com; p. 5 garanga/Shutterstock.com; p. 6 Jukka Palm/Shutterstock.com; p. 7 SJ
Travel Photo and Video/Shutterstock.com; pp. 8, 13 Homo Cosmicos/Shutterstock.com;
p. 9 Peter Hermes Furian/Shutterstock.com; p. 10 Guenter Albers/Shutterstock.com;
p. 11 AGF/Contributor/Universal Images Group/Getty Images; pp. 12, 20 De Agostini
Picture Library/Contributor/De Agostini/Getty Images; p. 14 nd3000/Shutterstock.com;
p. 15 Burger/Wikimedia Commons; p. 16 Culture Club/Contributor/Hulton Archive/
Getty Images; p. 17 Ras67/Wikimedia Commons; p. 18 Victoria Kurylo/Shutterstock.com;
p. 19 (grapes) Lukasz Szwaj/Shutterstock.com; p. 19 (olives) Studiovd/Shutterstock.com;
p. 19 (quince) nnattalli/Shutterstock.com; p. 19 (pears) Happy Lena/Shutterstock.com;
p. 19 (figs) simona pavan/Shutterstock.com; p. 21 (left) Marcella Medici/Wikimedia
Commons; p. 21 (right) Mikystar/Wikimedia Commons; p. 22 adoc-photos/Contributor/
Corbis Historical/Getty Images; p. 23 Archive Photos/Stringer/Archive Photos/Getty Images;
p. 24 Mirko Rizzotto/Wikimedia Commons; p. 25 Felistoria/Wikimedia Commons;
p. 26 Lakeview Images/Shutterstock.com; p. 27 Keystone-France/Contributor/
Gamma-Keystone/Getty Images; p. 29 VCG/Contributor/Visual China Group/Getty Images.

Printed in the United States of America

CPSIA compliance information: Batch #CS19GS: For further information contact Gareth Stevens, New York, New York at 1-800-542-2595.

CONTENTS

Words in the glossary appear in **bold** type the first time they are used in the text.

GORGEOUS GARDENS

You might have a vegetable garden in your backyard. Or you may have visited places with beautiful flower gardens. The Hanging Gardens of Babylon were likely very different from any garden you've ever seen!

In fact, this world wonder will definitely make you think differently about any gardens you know! Read on to learn about what the Hanging Gardens were, what kinds of plants were likely found there, and why there are **theories** about whether this amazing place even existed at all!

The gardens may have made
the ancient city of Babylon
even more beautiful.

BABYLON FACTS

FOR A TIME, BABYLON WAS THE LARGEST CITY IN THE WORLD.

Babylon began its great growth as a city in Mesopotamia during the 1700s BC. By the 600s BC, under the rule of King Nebuchadnezzar II, Babylon grew to 4 square miles (10 sq km)!

This ancient city, now in ruins, is also sometimes called Babel. It's written about in the Bible!

The Euphrates is the longest river in southwest Asia.

THE EUPHRATES RIVER FLOWED THROUGH THE MIDDLE OF BABYLON.

This was an advantage for a few reasons. It was an important water source for people to grow crops. It also was part of the large trade system of the Babylonians.

THE ANCIENT CITY OF BABYLON WAS LOCATED IN MODERN-DAY IRAQ.

Many **archaeologists** have worked to uncover parts of the city, but warfare in Iraq starting in 2003 made this harder. Many of the **sites** have been **damaged** or had things taken from them.

This statue of a lion is one of the most famous sites for people who visit the ruins of Babylon. Today, plans are in place to keep sites like this safe.

WHERE WAS BABYLON?

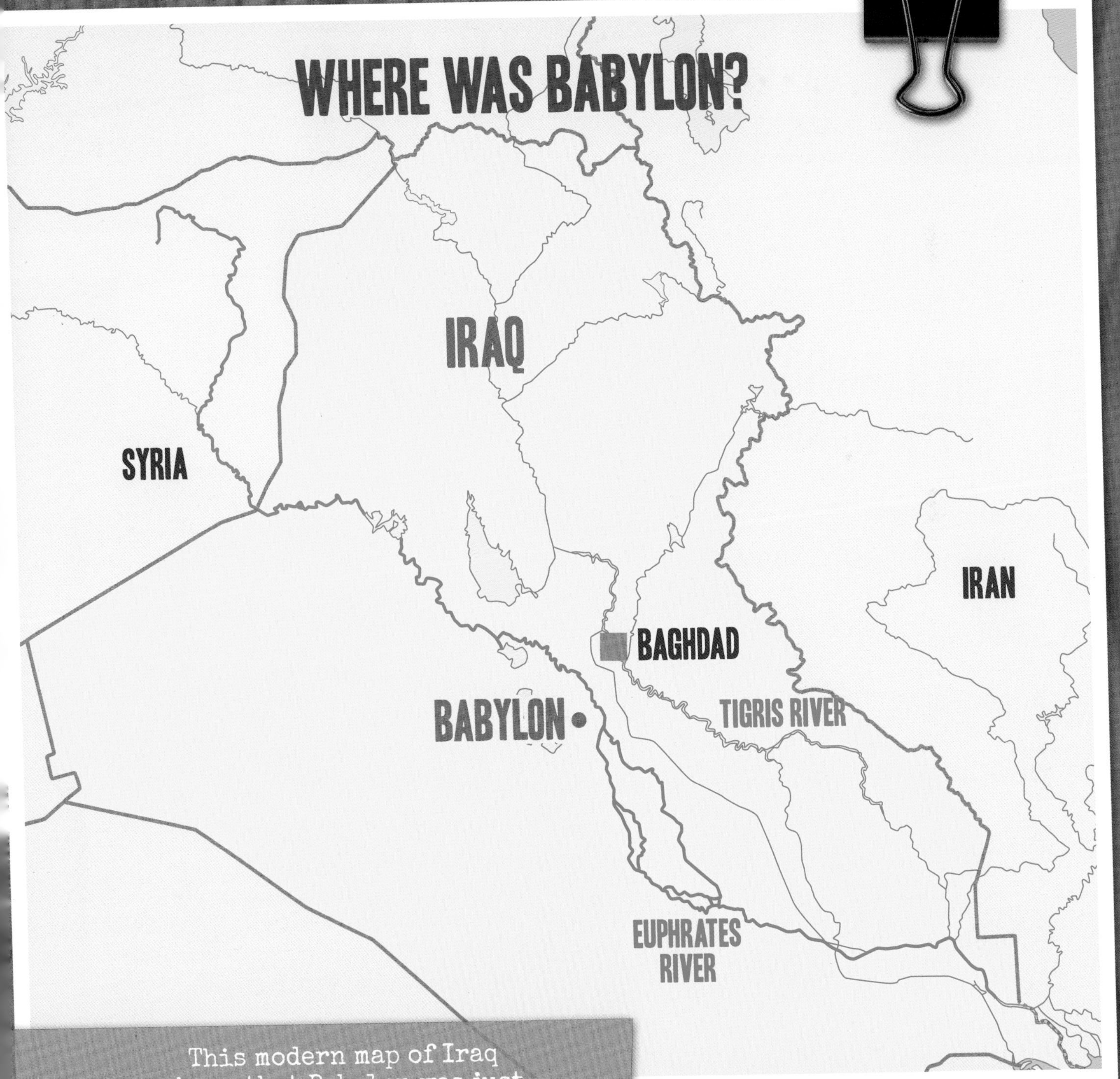

SYRIA

IRAQ

IRAN

BAGHDAD

BABYLON •

TIGRIS RIVER

EUPHRATES RIVER

This modern map of Iraq shows that Babylon was just south of where the city of Baghdad is today.

A WORLD WONDER

THE HANGING GARDENS ARE CONSIDERED ONE OF THE SEVEN WONDERS OF THE ANCIENT WORLD.

This means they're seen as one of the most impressive things ancient people ever created. Also on this list are the Pyramids of Giza in Egypt, the statue of Zeus at Olympia in Greece, and a lighthouse called the Pharos of Alexandria in Egypt.

GREAT PYRAMIDS OF GIZA

The Ishtar Gate was one of eight entrances into the city of Babylon. At nearly 40 feet (12 m) high, it was also quite a wonder!

THE GARDENS WEREN'T THE ONLY ACCOMPLISHMENT OF THE BABYLONIANS.

The city of Babylon was surrounded by high, long walls that were said to be 80 feet (24 m) thick! The walls were such an incredible structure they could have been considered an ancient world wonder, too.

GARDEN GURUS

THE PLANTS IN THE HANGING GARDENS PROBABLY DIDN'T TRULY HANG.

Most people think the plants only appeared to hang. The plants may have been grown to drape, or fall over the side, of many different heights of **terraces**. Or, they may have been rooftop gardens.

Some theories say the gardens were built as part of the royal palace.

IRAQ

THE GARDENS COULDN'T GROW ON THEIR OWN.

Babylon had a very hot, dry **climate**. There wouldn't have been much rain to water the gardens. The number of plants described in the gardens would have needed a lot of help to grow!

13

Today, **irrigation** systems use sprinklers and long hoses to keep fields watered.

THE GARDENS LIKELY HAD THEIR OWN IRRIGATION SYSTEM.

Ancient writings say that water from the Euphrates River was used to keep the plants watered. A well found in the ruins of the palace of Babylon may have been used to bring water up to the high terraces.

THE GARDENS WERE BUILT TO BE LEAKPROOF.

BITUMEN

The roofs of the gardens were made of many different kinds of matter, such as lead, reeds, and bitumen. Today, bitumen is often called asphalt. This is the black matter used on the top of roads!

THE GARDENS HAD A LOT OF SUPPORT.

Baked bricks were part of the terraces' construction. The whole of the garden was also said to have been held up by stone **columns** and bases. One ancient writer noted that tree roots grew into a high terrace, not the ground!

THE GARDENS WERE LIKELY BUILT AS DECORATION.

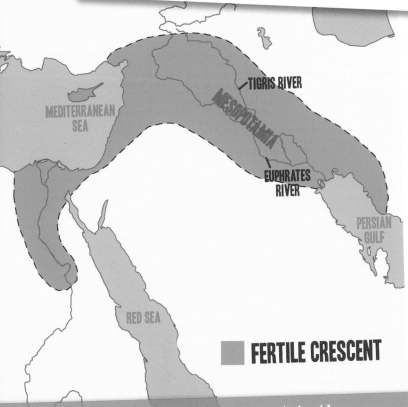

TIGRIS RIVER

MESOPOTAMIA

MEDITERRANEAN SEA

EUPHRATES RIVER

PERSIAN GULF

RED SEA

FERTILE CRESCENT

The Fertile Crescent is the area where the first farming communities in the Mediterranean and Middle East likely began. It's often called the "cradle of **civilization**."

Some historians believe the Hanging Gardens of Babylon were only meant to be beautiful. The idea that gardens could be created for pleasure probably began in the Fertile Crescent, where Babylon was located.

PLANTS IN THE GARDENS

FUN FACT: 12

ALMONDS MAY HAVE BEEN PLANTED IN THE HANGING GARDENS.

Wild almonds have been found by archaeologists in Greece that date back to 3000 BC. Since Greece is not far from present-day Iraq, it's possible that almonds were planted in the gardens!

ALMOND PLANT

PLANTS POSSIBLY FOUND IN THE HANGING GARDENS OF BABYLON

GRAPES

OLIVES

QUINCE

PEARS

FIGS

These are some of the plants that could have been found in the Hanging Gardens of Babylon based on where they grow and how long they've been grown by people.

SIZING UP THE GARDENS

THE GARDENS MAY HAVE BEEN UP TO 75 FEET (22.9 M) TALL IN PLACES.

That's about the height of four giraffes stacked on top of each other! Considering that these gardens needed to be watered and cared for just like any other garden, that's tall!

Diodorus was a Greek writer and historian who wrote a long history that included ancient **myths** and events through about 60 BC.

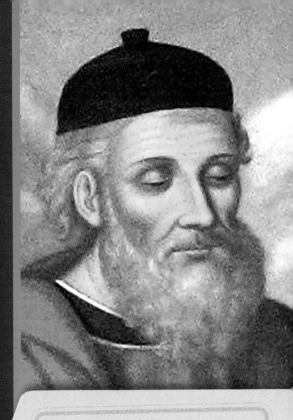

ΔΙΟΔΩΡΟΥ ΤΟΥ ΣΙΚΕΛΙΩΤΟΥ

ΒΙΒΛΙΟΘΗΚΗΣ ΙΣΤΟΡΙΚΗΣ

ΤΑ ΣΩΖΟΜΕΝΑ.

DIODORI SICULI

BIBLIOTHECAE HISTORICAE

LIBRI QUI SUPERSUNT,

INTERPRETE

LAURENTIO RHODOMANO.

AD FIDEM MSS. RECENSUIT

PETRUS WESSELINGIUS,

FUN FACT: 14

THE GARDENS MAY HAVE BEEN ABOUT 400 FEET (122 M) LONG ON EACH SIDE.

Diodorus of Sicily, who lived around 50 BC, wrote about the Hanging Gardens. In his writings, he described a garden with an incredibly long length that sloped like a hillside.

21

THE BUILDER

THE HANGING GARDENS OF BABYLON WERE PROBABLY BUILT AS A GIFT.

One story of the gardens is about Babylonian King Nebuchadnezzar II. He may have had the beautiful gardens built to please his wife, who greatly missed her homeland of Media.

King Nebuchadnezzar II ruled Babylon from about 605 BC to 561 BC.

SOME STORIES SAY THE GARDENS WERE BUILT BEFORE NEBUCHADNEZZAR'S RULE.

Sammu-ramat (or Semiramis) was queen of Assyria, an area very near where Babylon was built. Some historical accounts say she built the Hanging Gardens! There is less evidence for this story, however.

PROOF OF THE GARDENS?

ALL WRITINGS ABOUT THE GARDENS WERE WRITTEN AFTER BABYLON HAD BEEN ABANDONED!

No writings that tell of the building of the gardens have been discovered from Nebuchadnezzar II's time. This makes historians question when and where the gardens may have been built.

BEROSUS

The first **descriptions** of the gardens were written around 290 BC by a priest named Berosus who wrote three books in Greek about Babylon's history and culture, including the gardens.

While Koldewey unearthed some amazing Babylonian ruins, it's now thought the mysterious building he discovered was just a storehouse, not the gardens.

AN ARCHAEOLOGIST UNEARTHED THE GARDENS IN THE EARLY 1900s—OR DID HE?

Robert Koldewey began digging in southern Iraq in 1899. He spent 18 years there and discovered a temple, the city's great wall, and part of the Ishtar Gate. He believed he found the Hanging Gardens of Babylon, too!

Just like we aren't totally sure what the gardens looked like, we aren't completely sure where they were found!

THE GARDENS MAY NOT HAVE BEEN IN BABYLON!

Some historians believe the gardens were located in Babylon, but there are also people who believe they were located in a city called Nineveh. This was the capital of the Assyrian Empire.

THE HANGING GARDENS MAY NOT HAVE EVER EXISTED!

Whether or not the gardens existed isn't known right now, but exploring the ruins of Babylon may someday hold the answer to this mystery.

Archaeologists have never found any proven ruins of the gardens, even though many people wrote about them in ancient books and writings. The gardens are the only ancient wonder whose existence is uncertain among historians.

A MYSTERIOUS CREATION

The Hanging Gardens of Babylon are one fascinating piece of ancient history. Were they created as a gift? Did they even exist at all? Though there are still questions about their existence, the gardens can tell us a lot about the ancient civilization of Babylon.

Today, archaeologists continue their work of uncovering ancient ruins. One of their discoveries may someday hold the key to knowing more about this world wonder!

These newly constructed gardens in Shanghai, China, are built to look like what the Hanging Gardens of Babylon may have looked like.

GLOSSARY

archaeologist: a scientist who studies past human life and activities

civilization: organized society with written records and laws

climate: the average weather conditions of a place over a period of time

column: a tall, strong supporting post

damage: to cause harm

decoration: something that is added to something else to make it more attractive

description: a bit of writing that tells how something looks or sounds

irrigation: the watering of a dry area by man-made means in order to grow plants

myth: a story that was told by a people to explain a practice, belief, or natural event

site: the place where something is, was, or will be located

terrace: a flat area created on the side of a hill and used especially for growing crops

theory: an explanation based on facts that is generally accepted by scientists

FOR MORE INFORMATION

BOOKS

Bergin, Mark. *Wonders of the World*. Jonesville, MI: Book House, 2015.

Wood, Alix. *Uncovering the Culture of Ancient Mesopotamia*. New York, NY: PowerKids Press, 2016.

WEBSITES

Hanging Gardens of Babylon
www.dkfindout.com/us/history/seven-wonders-world/hanging-gardens-babylon/
Check out more about the Hanging Gardens of Babylon and other wonders of the ancient world.

King Hammurabi
kidspast.com/world-history/hammurabi-babylonian-empire/
Learn about one of the most infamous rulers in the ancient world on this interactive site.

INDEX